PUDDINGS
CUSTARDS AND FLANS

PUDDINGS
CUSTARDS AND FLANS

**43 EASY RECIPES
FROM OLD FAVORITES
TO NEW CREATIONS**

LINDA ZIMMERMAN

Clarkson Potter/Publishers
New York

Published by Clarkson N. Potter, Inc., 201 East 50th Street, New
York, New York 10022. Member of the Crown Publishing Group.

CLARKSON N. POTTER, POTTER, and colophon are
trademarks of Clarkson N. Potter, Inc.

Manufactured in the United States of America

Library of Congress Cataloging-in-Publication Data
Zimmerman, Linda.
Puddings, custards, and flans: 43 easy recipes—from old favorites to
new creations/Linda Zimmerman.—1st ed.
1. Puddings. 2. Desserts. I. Title.
TX773.Z55   1990
641.8′64—dc20   90-32640
CIP

ISBN 0-517-57443-8

Design by Barbara Kantor

1   3   5   7   9   10   8   6   4   2

First Edition

For
Lou Zimmerman and Doug Arango

CONTENTS

INTRODUCTION

I discovered the joy of eating pudding in the 1950s. My mother always seemed to have an endless supply of small, short-stemmed custard cups filled with creamy chocolate, butterscotch, or vanilla pudding lurking in the refrigerator, just waiting for a hungry kid. One of my favorite treats was a silken dark chocolate pudding, which could only be improved upon when I topped it with squiggles of whipped cream squirted from a can.

I also ravenously devoured puddings I didn't even know were puddings—a delectable potato kugel that is still my favorite dish, and noodle kugel, a sweet marriage of broad egg noodles with raisins, apples, and cinnamon and bound with beaten eggs, sour cream, and cream cheese. Served as side dishes, these kugels were for some reason special-occasion or brunch food.

When I first thought about writing a book devoted to puddings, I had no idea just what a delicious mess I was getting myself into. Of course, I knew about bread puddings, rice puddings, and steamed puddings. But as I investigated further, I discovered a bounty of assorted puddings, mainly in cookbooks written prior to the 1930s, when these dishes seemed to be at the height of their popularity. Most astonishing were the nearly two hundred recipes given in *Mrs. Beeton's Household Management*, first published in England in 1861.

This book represents a small cross section of all those inviting dishes of various textures and tastes known as puddings.

Pudding is really a vague generic term. *Larousse Gastronomique* defines pudding as "any of numerous dishes, sweet or savoury, served hot or cold, which are prepared in a variety of ways." In Great Britain *pudding* usually refers to any dessert, while in America puddings are more narrowly limited to sweet, creamy, custardlike concoctions that are baked or cooked on top of the stove, or to moist, cakelike steamed puddings. But there are also wonderful uncooked puddings, as well as myriad savory puddings that serve as side dishes or light meals in themselves.

However puddings are cooked, they have one thing in common: they taste delicious. And they have been popping up with recurring frequency on more and more menus, no longer considered merely little kids' nursery food or too unglamorous for company.

For this book, I have chosen what I consider the best recipes from hundreds of possibilities and have organized them into five categories.

Baked puddings, those that are finished in the oven, include homey rice puddings, traditional · puddings such as New England's favorite Indian Pudding and Great Britain's well-loved Queen of Lemon Meringue Pudding, such special-occasion puddings as Chocolate Hazelnut Sponge Pudding, and a variety of bread puddings.

Steamed puddings evoke thoughts of Charles Dickens and winter holidays. And, true, you will find a Christmas Plum Pudding here, but Cherry and Almond Pudding and Black-and-White Marble Pudding both are desserts you can serve any time of the year.

Stove-top puddings are those that are first cooked in a pot on top of the stove. Most take only minutes to prepare. Mrs. Donaldson's English Rice Pudding is the best rice pudding I've ever eaten. For berry lovers and weight watchers, Angel Food Summer Pudding, one of the easiest to prepare, provides a light ending to a summer meal, as does the berry-laden Rote Grütze.

Savory puddings offer Brie and Crab Strata, a scrumptious 1990s' update of a classical 1960s' casserole, and three variations of Yorkshire Pudding, as well as Green Corn Tamale Pudding and Tex-Mex Polenta Mini-Puddings, two unique dishes incorporating basic southwestern ingredients.

Custards and flans include an easy basic Baked Vanilla Custard and Crème Brûlée and more sophisticated recipes, such as Mascarpone Cheesecake Flan, Frozen White Chocolate Pots de Crème, and Pear and Ginger Custard.

You'll also find a section of toppings and sauces, such as Crème Anglaise, Crème Fraîche, Caramel Sauce, and Helen's Never-Fail Fudge Sauce, that can be used to complement any number of puddings and custards.

Most puddings and custards are easy to prepare, requiring no great culinary skill and no special equipment. They usually are made with the basic ingredients on hand in the kitchen. Combinations of flavors, ingredients, and textures are limited only by one's imagination, so feel free to experiment.

STEAMED PUDDINGS

Steamed puddings are easy to assemble: the ingredients are simply mixed together and poured into a prepared mold. The secret to making light steamed puddings is the use of bread crumbs in addition to or instead of flour. Steamed puddings that are not to be served immediately can be frozen or stored in the refrigerator (which allows their flavors the time to blend) and resteamed before serving.

PUDDING MOLDS

Pudding molds are worthwhile investments. Available in cookware stores or by mail order, most are relatively inexpensive and will last for years.

Metal molds come in various sizes and shapes, but they have two things in common: a tube in the center, which promotes even cooking from within, and a tight-fitting lid with a handle, which is usually secured to the mold by two or three metal clips. Although these molds are designed specifically for steaming, they can also be used to create beautiful molded cold desserts. Most of the steamed puddings in this book were cooked in metal pudding molds.

Glazed ceramic pudding bowls, available in an assortment of sizes, produce the dome-shaped "puds" so commonly referred to in most turn-of-the-century cookbooks. When a ceramic bowl is used for steaming, the pudding must first be sealed with pleated baking parchment or foil that has been buttered on both sides. A cotton pudding cloth is then draped over the top of the pudding. The bowl's distinguishing inch-wide basin rim functions as a lip to which the pudding cloth can be secured by string. The ends of the cloth are then brought up diagonally and tied securely in a knot on top.

Coffee cans, both the 1- and 2-pound sizes, make acceptable and very inexpensive molds. Tightly seal the pudding with buttered heavy foil before steaming. The cans must be thoroughly washed and dried after each use so they don't rust.

HOW TO STEAM PUDDINGS

Pudding molds and their lids should be generously greased and then dusted with sugar before the molds are filled. For a 3-cup mold, use 2 to 3 teaspoons butter and 2 teaspoons sugar; for a 1½-quart mold, use 3 to 4 teaspoons butter and 4 teaspoons sugar; and for a 2- or 3-quart mold, use 1½ to 2 tablespoons butter and 2 to 3 tablespoons sugar.

I use butter because I like the taste, but margarine, flavorless cooking oil, or any solid vegetable shortening can be used. To cut down on calories, use a nonstick vegetable spray and eliminate the sugar.

A flour dredger filled with granulated sugar is an easy way to dust the mold. Rotate the mold as you sprinkle the sugar, to ensure that the sides and the tube are completely dusted.

Fill the mold from two-thirds to three-fourths full, providing adequate space between the lid and the batter to allow the pudding to rise and expand as it steams. After the mold is filled, tap it on a counter several times to break up any air bubbles, then secure the lid.

For steaming, use any deep, heavy pot, such as a spaghetti pot, lobster pot, or stockpot, with a tight-fitting lid. The pot has to be large enough to let steam circulate around the mold.

Place a small steaming rack, a trivet, or even a folded dish towel on the bottom of the pot for the mold to sit on. Under no circumstances do you want the mold to rest directly on the bottom of the pot. Place the unfilled mold on the rack and pour enough water into the pot to reach about halfway to two-thirds up the mold. Remove the mold and set the pot to boil. Fill the mold and carefully lower onto the rack when the water starts to boil. Cover the pot and steam the pudding for the required length of time. Make sure the water is always lightly bubbling at an even simmer. Keep a kettle of boiling water at hand to maintain an even water level in the pot while the pudding is steaming. Check the pudding at half-hour intervals. Always wear heavy potholder mittens when you check the water level or when handling the hot pudding mold. When you lift the pot lid, tilt the far edge up and toward you so that the lid shields you from escaping steam.

To check if the pudding is done, remove the mold to a rack on the counter, unfasten the lid, and insert a bamboo skewer or sharp knife in or near the center of the pudding. The skewer should come out with a few crumbs sticking to it. To serve hot, let the pudding rest on a rack for about 10 minutes, or until the pudding shrinks away from the sides of the mold. Invert it onto a serving plate. The pudding will stay warm for several hours if you do not remove it from the mold.

Pressure cookers. I have had great success steaming puddings in my pressure cooker. The secret is to steam the pudding for 30 minutes in the cooker before allowing the pressure to build, then set the pressure gauge. Start timing when the required pressure has been reached. With this method, steamed puddings can be made in half the usual time. Always follow the manufacturer's directions for your pressure cooker, since all brands are different.

FREEZING STEAMED PUDDINGS

Steamed puddings can be frozen for months. They can be kept in their molds if they are to be frozen for less than two weeks, but I prefer unmolding them first. Wrap the unmolded pudding in heavy aluminum foil or a double layer of plastic wrap and seal in an airtight freezer bag.

REHEATING STEAMED PUDDINGS

Defrost the pudding overnight in the refrigerator. If it was frozen unmolded, carefully replace it in the mold or wrap it in lightly buttered foil. Steam on a rack for 1 to 2 hours, depending on the size of the pudding. You can also reheat the pudding in a bain-marie (see page 9) in the oven or in a microwave (in which case place the pudding on a plate and cover with plastic wrap). If using a microwave, remember that the heating time will vary depending on the wattage of your oven as well as the size of the pudding.

CUSTARDS AND FLANS

Dessert custards are the simplest of cooked puddings and are deceptively quick and easy to prepare. Made from a combination of milk and eggs to which sugar and some flavoring have been added, custards are characterized by their delicate flavor and smooth, velvety texture. They can be as rich as Crème Brûlée or as light and soothing as flan.

According to the American Egg Board, the minimum egg-to-milk ratio for a properly thickened custard is 1 egg and 2 tablespoons of sugar for each cup of milk. Adding more sugar will result in a softer custard, requiring longer cooking. A firmer custard can be achieved by increasing the amount of whole eggs to milk. Adding more eggs to the custard shortens the cooking time. A smoother custard is obtained by substituting 2 egg yolks for 1 whole egg. Two egg whites can also be substituted for 1 whole egg, but there will be a marked difference in the custard's flavor and color.

BEATING THE EGGS AND MILK

Lightly beat eggs with a whisk, eggbeater, or electric mixer just until blended, then lightly mix them into the milk. Always strain the mixture into a saucepan or custard mold. If a froth has formed from overbeating, skim it off before baking the custard.

COOKING OR BAKING CUSTARDS

Stirred custards, prepared by continuously stirring the ingredients over low heat until they are sufficiently thickened to coat the back of a metal spoon, are also referred to as soft custards (the pastry cream in Yankee Banana-Gingersnap Pudding), custard sauces (Crème Anglaise) and sometimes as boiled custards, a misleading reference since a custard must never boil. These custards require constant watching. Overcooking will cause the custard to break and the eggs to curdle. Delicate as they are, it is not necessary to prepare stirred custards in a double boiler so long as they are heated in a heavy saucepan over a low flame. Or you can use a flame diffuser to control the speed of the cooking. Stirred custards are pourable custards that thicken slightly as they cool.

Baked custards require less attention than stirred custards, jiggle when first removed from the oven, and have a firmer, more gelatinous texture. Bake them in ovenproof porcelain or glass cups or molds. I always bake them in a bain-marie, which is simply a hot-water bath that ensures slow, even cooking and a creamy texture. The dish containing the custard or pudding is placed in a heavy pan or pot filled with enough boiling water to reach halfway up the sides of the dish.

Flans are inverted custards (known in France as crème renversée) that are baked in a mold lined with caramelized sugar. The caramelized sugar liquefies as the custard bakes, forming a light sauce, which allows for easier unmolding of the custard.

HOW TO FIX A CURDLED CUSTARD

When a soft custard is not constantly stirred, or is cooked over too-high heat or cooked too long, it will either become lumpy—resembling scrambled eggs—or begin to curdle. It can usually be rescued if the curdling has not progressed too far. Immediately remove the custard from the heat and slowly pour it into a running blender or food processor. Blend about a minute, or until smooth.

HOW TO TEST BAKED CUSTARD FOR DONENESS

Custard continues to cook after being removed from the oven, so it is important not to overbake it. Custard is done when a clean knife inserted near, but not in, the center comes out clean. The center will be slightly wobbly when the custard is removed from the oven. As the custard cools, it will set. When baked in cups, each custard should be checked for doneness.

HOW TO COOL CUSTARD

This is an important step, since the cooking process must be stopped as soon as the custard is removed from the heat.

Stirred custard should be cooled to room temperature by gentle stirring with a wooden spoon for 30 to 40 seconds to release the steam. Even better, place the saucepan in a bowl of ice water while you stir.

Baked custard should be immediately removed from the bain-marie and set on a rack to cool to room temperature before refrigeration.

STORING CUSTARD

Custards and flans should be room temperature before they are lightly covered with wax paper or plastic wrap and refrigerated. Custard is usually best served the day it is made, or within two days of its preparation. Unless called for, do not freeze custards.

INGREDIENTS

Eggs. Large eggs have been used in all of the recipes in this book, but you can substitute equal numbers of extra-large or medium eggs without noticeably different results. You can use whole eggs straight from the refrigerator. If the recipe calls for beaten egg whites, always bring the eggs to room temperature first.

Milk and cream. The higher the fat content in the custard, the silkier the texture. You can replace whole milk with low-fat milk (1% or 2% milk) and substitute light cream or half-and-half for heavy cream in all of the pudding and custard recipes. Do not use nonfat milk (skim milk) in the custards.

Even though raw or pasteurized cream is harder to find in the markets, try to use it instead of ultrapasteurized cream with its longer shelf life. Ultrapasteurized cream will work with these recipes, but it imparts an unpleasant, bitter aftertaste.

Burnt sugar for crème brûlée. There are several different ways to obtain a good burnt sugar topping. The most common method is to sprinkle the required amount of sugar on top of the custard, set the custard under a preheated broiler (about 4 inches below the flame), and let the sugar caramelize, being careful that it doesn't burn. Be sure to use a dish that will not crack or shatter when exposed to high heat.

Sugar can also be melted separately under a preheated broiler on a buttered sheet of heavy aluminum foil. Place the foil on a cookie sheet. Trace the shape of the bottom of the custard dish on the foil with the tip of a pen; don't use a knife or other sharp utensil. Butter the traced shape, then sprinkle on the sugar. If using brown sugar, press the sugar through a strainer. Broil until the sugar has melted to the desired color. Watch carefully so it doesn't burn. Let the sugar cool and harden on the foil, then lift it from the foil and place on the custard.

Another method is to use a salamander, an inexpensive and useful French utensil made expressly for glazing the top of prepared food. It resembles a thick metal hockey puck attached to a long heavy steel rod. Used like a branding iron, the round end is inserted into the flame on the stove until it is red hot, then lightly pressed on top of the sugar until the sugar caramelizes to golden brown.

Caramelized sugar. Caramelization is merely the melting of granulated sugar over low heat until it liquefies and turns pale golden brown.

Mix the sugar and water together in a heavy nonreactive pan (do not use aluminum) and stir over low heat. The sugar will start to bubble around the sides of the pan and then come to a boil. As the water evaporates, the sugar crystallizes and begins to melt. Using a long-handled wooden spoon, stir the melting sugar just until it turns a clear, pale amber. This will take about 10 to 15 minutes, depending on the amount of sugar used. Do not allow the sugar to become too dark—overcooking or burning will make it bitter. Remove from the heat immediately and, working very quickly, pour the caramel into ungreased custard cups or a mold. Tilt the cups or mold as you pour to completely coat the bottom and sides. The caramel will harden almost immediately.

BAKED PUDDINGS

OLD-FASHIONED RICE PUDDING

This is a very easy version of an old favorite.

SERVES 6

1 to 2 tablespoons unsalted butter

1 large egg

1 cup half-and-half

3 cups milk

½ cup sugar

¼ cup long-grain white rice

⅓ cup raisins or currants

1 teaspoon vanilla extract

Ground cinnamon

Ground nutmeg

Heavy cream

Preheat the oven to 300° F. Lightly butter a shallow 1½-quart Pyrex baking dish.

Lightly beat the egg and half-and-half in a 2-quart bowl. Add the milk, sugar, rice, raisins, and vanilla. Mix well and pour into the baking dish. Stirring occasionally, bake for 2½ to 3 hours, or until the liquid is absorbed and the pudding is set.

Sprinkle the top with cinnamon and nutmeg. Serve warm or chilled, with cold heavy cream.

INDIAN PUDDING

Indian pudding is the definitive Yankee dessert. By replacing the flour or oatmeal in hasty pudding with the much cheaper and readily available Indian corn, the early New England settlers created this unpretentious and beloved pudding. Don't cheat on the long cooking time necessary to produce the authentic texture.

SERVES 6

4 tablespoons unsalted butter

3 cups milk

½ cup yellow cornmeal

1 large egg, lightly beaten

¼ cup dark molasses

¼ cup maple syrup

¼ cup firmly packed dark brown sugar

½ teaspoon ground ginger

⅛ teaspoon salt

Vanilla ice cream or Maple Caramelized
    Pecans (page 108)

Preheat the oven to 300° F. Butter a 2-quart ceramic pudding bowl or deep 2-quart baking dish with 2 tablespoons butter.

In a medium saucepan, scald 2½ cups milk over medium-high heat. Lower the heat to medium and whisk in the cornmeal slowly so no lumps form. Cook, stirring constantly with a wooden spoon, just until the mixture begins to thicken. Stir in the egg, then the molasses, syrup, sugar, ginger, and salt. Bring to a boil, stirring constantly. Lower the heat and continue cooking and stirring until the mixture is very thick and pulls away from the sides of the pan. Remove from the heat and stir in the remaining butter.

Scrape the mixture into the baking dish. Bake for an hour, then lower the heat to 275° F. Pour the remaining milk over the pudding and bake for an additional 4 to 5 hours, or until the pudding is firm. Serve very warm, topped with vanilla ice cream or Maple Caramelized Pecans.

TURTLE PUDDING

If you love sticky buns and pecan rolls, you'll love Turtle Pudding.

1½ tablespoons unsalted butter

10 slices day-old white bread, cut into
cubes

1¾ cups milk

½ cup heavy cream

½ cup sugar

2 tablespoons applesauce

3 large eggs

2 teaspoons vanilla extract

1 tablespoon dark rum

½ cup chopped pecans

½ cup mini bittersweet chocolate chips

1 cup Caramel Sauce (page 102), or ⅓
to ½ cup Caramel Sauce and ½ cup
Helen's Never-Fail Fudge Sauce
(page 106), heated

Butter a 2-quart square or oblong ovenproof glass baking dish.

Put the bread cubes in a large bowl. In another bowl, beat together the milk, cream, sugar, applesauce, eggs, vanilla, and rum. Pour over the bread. Stir in the pecans and chocolate chips. Pour the pudding into the baking dish, and pour on ⅓ to ½ cup Caramel Sauce. Let sit for half an hour or more (the longer bread puddings sit, the better the flavor and texture).

Preheat oven to 350° F. and bake for 45 to 50 minutes. The pudding will be very puffy when done. Let it settle for 10 to 15 minutes before cutting. Serve warm with the remaining Caramel Sauce or with Helen's Never-Fail Fudge Sauce.

CHOCOLATE PRALINE
CROISSANT PUDDING

Y*ou can't count calories while eating this pudding.*

SERVES 6 TO 8

1½ to 2 tablespoons unsalted butter

4 3-ounce croissants

6 ounces semisweet chocolate

1 cup milk

1 cup half-and-half

2 large eggs

1 large egg yolk

2 tablespoons Kahlúa or other coffee
    liqueur

2 teaspoons vanilla extract

¼ cup sugar

1 cup crushed Praline (page 108)

Whipped cream

Lightly butter an 8 x 8 x 2-inch ovenproof glass baking dish.

Tear the croissants into large chunks and place in a large bowl. Set aside.

In a heavy saucepan, melt the chocolate in the milk over low heat. In a bowl, lightly beat together the half-and-half, eggs, egg yolk, Kahlúa, vanilla, and sugar, then whisk into the chocolate milk. Pour over the croissant pieces. Let sit for 10 minutes.

With a slotted spoon, carefully transfer half the croissants to the baking dish. Sprinkle on half of the Praline. Layer with the remaining croissants, and lightly pat to smooth top. Pour the custard the croissants soaked in over the pudding, and sprinkle with the remaining Praline. Let sit for at least 45 minutes, or overnight.

Preheat the oven to 350° F. and bake for 45 to 55 minutes, or until the pudding is set and puffy. Serve warm or chilled, with whipped cream.

APPLE CAPIROTADA

*C*lassic American apple pie fixings are combined in this robust variation of Mexican bread pudding, equally delicious for Sunday brunch or dessert.

SERVES 10

2 to 3 tablespoons unsalted butter

3 cups heavy cream

1 cup firmly packed brown sugar

1 cup water

1 cinnamon stick

3 cloves

1 1-pound day-old French or Italian
　　bread, cut into 1-inch-thick slices
　　(about 14 slices)

2 medium green pippin apples, cored,
　　peeled, and thinly sliced

¾ cup golden raisins

¾ cup chopped pecans

½ pound sharp Cheddar cheese,
　　shredded

4 large eggs

Ground cinnamon

Whipped cream or Crème Anglaise
　　(page 99)

Preheat the oven to 350° F. Butter a 3-quart oblong baking dish.

Scald the cream in a medium saucepan. Set aside to cool to room temperature. In another saucepan, combine the sugar, water, cinnamon stick, and cloves. Simmer gently for 5 minutes. Remove from the heat and let cool to room temperature. Mix with 2 cups of the cream.

Meanwhile, place the bread slices on a cookie sheet and lightly toast for about 10 minutes, just until dry but not browned. Cut into large cubes and place in a large bowl. Strain the cream mixture over the bread. Let stand for 10 to 20 minutes, or until the bread has thoroughly absorbed the liquid.

Layer half of the bread in the baking dish. Add layers of apples, raisins, pecans, and cheese.

With a whisk, beat the eggs with the remaining cream and pour half into the baking dish. Add the rest of the bread, and pour on the remaining egg mixture. Press down with your hand to make sure all the bread becomes thoroughly saturated. Let sit for half an hour or more

Bake in a bain-marie in a preheated 350° F. oven for 50 minutes to 1 hour, or until the pudding puffs up and turns brown and crusty. Let cool for about 20 minutes. Sprinkle with a dusting of cinnamon, and top with whipped cream or Crème Anglaise.

PEACHY BREAD PUDDING
WITH BLUEBERRY SAUCE

This *light, summery bread pudding provides an inviting contrast of flavors and colors. The pudding will keep for several days in the refrigerator. Bring it to room temperature before serving so the flavors can develop.*

SERVES 10 TO 12

- 10 tablespoons (1¼ sticks) unsalted butter
- 3 tablespoons plus ¾ cup sugar
- 3 cups milk
- 1 cup half-and-half
- 6 large eggs
- 1 cup bottled peach nectar
- 2 teaspoons vanilla extract
- 1 pound fresh peaches, peeled and coarsely chopped (about 2 cups)
- 10 cups 1-inch bread cubes from a day-old 1-pound egg bread or challah (about 10 to 12 slices)
- 2 cups Blueberry Sauce (page 103), warmed

Garnish

> 1 very large peach, unpeeled but cut
> into 10 to 12 slices just before
> serving
>
> 1 pint blueberries

Butter a 12-cup bundt pan with 2 tablespoons butter. Dust the sides with 3 tablespoons sugar.

Combine the milk, half-and-half, and remaining butter in a medium saucepan and bring just to a boil, allowing the butter to melt. Let cool slightly. In a bowl, beat the eggs with the peach nectar, remaining sugar, and vanilla. Stir into the milk mixture.

In a large mixing bowl, toss the peaches with the bread cubes. Pour the milk mixture over and mix thoroughly. Let sit for at least 30 minutes so the bread absorbs all the liquid.

Preheat the oven to 350° F. Add the pudding to the bundt pan. Bake in a bain-marie for about 1 hour, or until firm.

Let cool for at least 1 hour before serving. Nap each serving plate with Blueberry Sauce, and garnish with peach slices and blueberries.

JEM'S NEW ORLEANS BREAD AND BUTTER PUDDING

Everyone will ask for this deceptively simple recipe, which is based on an old New Orleans standard.

SERVES 4

1 cup milk

1 3-inch piece of vanilla bean, split

4 tablespoons unsalted butter

2 slices white bread, lightly toasted

2 large eggs

½ cup sugar

⅔ cup raisins

Ground cinnamon

Ground nutmeg

Whipped cream

Preheat the oven to 350° F.

Combine the milk and vanilla bean in a small saucepan. Scald the milk over medium heat. Remove from the heat and let the vanilla bean steep for 10 minutes.

Melt the butter in a 1½-quart ovenproof glass baking dish in the oven for 5 to 10 minutes. Tear the toast into large pieces and toss in the melted butter.

In a bowl, beat the eggs with the sugar until pale yellow.

Remove the vanilla bean from the milk and stir in the egg mixture. Strain over the bread, sprinkle with raisins, and dust with cinnamon and nutmeg.

Bake in a bain-marie for 35 minutes, or until a knife inserted in the center comes out clean. Serve warm or chilled, with whipped cream.

QUEEN OF LEMON
MERINGUE PUDDING

Queen of Pudding is one of the best-known traditional English puddings. In this variation, tangy lemon curd creates a tartlike pudding perfect for an afternoon tea break.

SERVES 5 TO 6

1 medium lemon

2½ cups milk

½ cup fine dry bread crumbs

2 large eggs, separated

1 large whole egg

⅓ cup plus 2 tablespoons sugar

1 teaspoon vanilla extract

½ cup Lemon Curd (page 100)

Preheat the oven to 350° F.

With a potato peeler, peel the zest from the lemon, making sure no white pith is included. Combine the milk with the zest in a medium saucepan and scald over medium-high heat. Remove from the heat and let sit for 10 minutes.

Put the bread crumbs in a mixing bowl. Lightly beat together the egg yolks and whole egg. When the milk has cooled, discard the zest and mix in the ⅓ cup sugar, the vanilla, and the eggs. Pour over the bread crumbs and stir to moisten all the crumbs. Pour into an 8- or 9-inch pie pan. Bake for 30 to 35 minutes, or until a knife inserted in the center comes out clean.

Gently spread a layer of Lemon Curd over the pudding. Beat the egg whites with the remaining sugar until stiff peaks form. Spread the meringue over the Lemon Curd. Bake for 5 to 8 minutes, or until the meringue is lightly browned. Serve warm, in wedges.

VARIATION

Substitute ½ cup strawberry or raspberry jam for the lemon curd.

CHOCOLATE HAZELNUT
SPONGE PUDDING

Based on a recipe from my friend chef Gerri Gilliland, this is a rich pudding that forms its own sauce. Be forewarned, a little goes a long way.

SERVES 6 TO 8

2 tablespoons unsalted butter

Sauce

¾ cup firmly packed light brown sugar

½ cup Dutch cocoa

¼ cup good bourbon

1¼ cups boiling water

Sponge

6 ounces semisweet chocolate

¾ cup (1½ sticks) unsalted butter

4 large egg yolks

¾ cup granulated sugar

2 teaspoons Frangelico (Italian hazelnut liqueur)

1 teaspoon vanilla extract

⅛ teaspoon salt

½ cup ground toasted hazelnuts (filberts)

¼ cup all-purpose flour

5 large egg whites

Hazelnut Whipped Cream (page 107)

Preheat the oven to 350° F. Grease a 10- or 11-inch round cake pan with 3-inch-deep sides with 2 tablespoons butter.

Mix the brown sugar, cocoa, bourbon, and boiling water and pour into the pan. (Add another ¼ cup boiling water if you prefer more sauce.) This makes a lot of liquid, but you'll find that it works.

Over low heat, melt the chocolate and butter in the top of a double boiler. Set aside to cool. In a medium bowl, beat the egg yolks with ½ cup sugar until they are pale yellow. Add the melted chocolate, Frangelico, vanilla, and salt. Mix in the nuts and flour until they are thoroughly moistened.

Beat the egg whites with the remaining sugar until stiff. Gently fold into the batter.

Carefully spoon the batter over the sauce in the pan. Bake for 35 to 45 minutes. The pudding is done when firm, with a cracked, shiny crust. The sauce may be bubbly and boiling up around the sides. Let the pudding cool for 20 minutes, or until the bubbling subsides and the sponge has fallen slightly.

Using a flexible metal spatula or knife, loosen the pudding from the sides of the pan, making sure none sticks. Carefully invert the pudding onto a platter large enough to catch all the sauce, which will be very thin. Serve the pudding warm with sauce spooned over and accompanied by Hazelnut Whipped Cream. Or chill the pudding overnight; it will absorb all the sauce, for a dessert similar to dense flourless chocolate cake.

PEACH AND CHERRY CLAFOUTIS

*C*lafoutis *is a sweet batter pudding that originated in Limousin, France. It is perfect for Sunday brunch.*

SERVES 6 TO 8

2½ tablespoons unsalted butter

¾ cup all-purpose flour

3 large eggs

¾ cup sugar

1 cup milk

2 tablespoons Kirsch

2 teaspoons vanilla extract

¼ teaspoon salt

3 medium peaches, peeled and sliced
    (1½ cups)

2 cups sweet black cherries, pitted
    (about 1⅓ pounds)

¾ cup Crème Fraîche (page 101)

Preheat the oven to 375° F. Melt the butter in a 10-inch deep-dish Pyrex pie pan in the oven.

In a food processor or blender, combine the flour, eggs, ½ cup sugar, milk, Kirsch, vanilla, and salt. Process until well mixed. The batter will be thin.

When the butter is completely melted, quickly spread it over the bottom of the pan, either with a pastry brush or by tilting the pan from side to side. Pour in the batter. Strew the peaches on top, then add the cherries, making sure the fruit is well incorporated in the batter. Sprinkle the remaining sugar on top. Bake for 45 to 55 minutes, or until the clafoutis is golden brown and puffy. The pudding will fall a bit as it cools. Serve hot or warm with Crème Fraîche, or at room temperature.

STEAMED PUDDINGS

CHRISTMAS
PLUM PUDDING

Butter replaces the suet traditionally used for the sake of cooking time and certainly convenience. This pudding can be made three months prior to the holidays and left to age. It can also be served the day it is made.

SERVES 10 TO 15

1½ tablespoons plus ½ cup (1 stick)
   unsalted butter, softened
2 tablespoons granulated sugar
1½ cups diced mixed dried fruit
   (apples, peaches, pears, raisins,
   apricots, etc.)
1 cup golden raisins
½ cup currants
½ cup candied fruits
1 cup stewed prunes, drained, pitted,
   and chopped, or 8 ounces canned
   moist pitted prunes, chopped
1 medium tart apple, peeled, cored, and
   grated
Grated zest of 1 medium lemon
Grated zest of 1 medium orange
¼ cup orange juice

⅔ cup chopped pecans

¼ cup Armagnac or any high-quality
   brandy

¾ cup firmly packed brown sugar

3 large eggs

1 cup dry bread crumbs

½ cup all-purpose flour

1 teaspoon baking powder

1½ teaspoons ground cinnamon

1 teaspoon freshly grated nutmeg

½ teaspoon ground cloves

¼ teaspoon ground cardamom

¼ teaspoon salt

½ cup dark beer or milk

¼ to ½ cup (or to your liking) Rum or
   brandy for flaming

2 cups Rum Butter (page 105)

Butter the sides and lid of a 2- or 3-quart pudding mold with
the 1½ tablespoons butter. Dust the entire mold with the granulated sugar. Prepare a pot for steaming (see page 6). Combine
the dried fruit, raisins, currants, candied fruits, prunes, apple,
lemon and orange zest, orange juice, pecans, and Armagnac in
a large bowl. Mix well.

Cream remaining butter with brown sugar in mixer on medium
speed, or in a food processor, until light and fluffy. Beat in the
eggs, one at a time, until the mixture is very fluffy.

Combine the bread crumbs, flour, baking powder, cinnamon, nutmeg, cloves, cardamom, and salt. Stir into the egg mixture. Mix well. Mix in the beer and pour over the fruit mixture. Stir to completely combine. Spoon into the mold and secure the lid on the mold. Tap the mold on a counter to settle the pudding.

Steam the pudding on a rack over boiling water for 3½ to 4½ hours, checking the water level about every half an hour. Add boiling water as necessary if using two 1½-quart molds, cut the steaming time to 2½ to 3 hours.

Let the mold cool on a rack for 5 to 10 minutes, or until the pudding shrinks away from the sides. With the blunt edge of a knife, carefully loosen the pudding before unmolding. Invert onto a serving platter. Warm the rum in a small saucepan (do not let it boil). Light the rum and pour over the pudding. When the flames die, cut the pudding into slices and serve with Rum Butter.

To store pudding made in advance: Let cool in the mold for 10 minutes, unmold, and let cool to room temperature. Wrap the pudding in several layers of cheesecloth that has been soaked in rum or brandy, then wrap tightly in plastic wrap. Store in a cool, dry place. Check the pudding periodically, and sprinkle with additional rum or brandy if the cloth seems a little dry. This pudding also can be refrigerated for 3 months.

N O T E: To shorten the steaming time, this pudding can be made in a pressure cooker. Steam the pudding for 30 minutes before bringing to high pressure and cook for 2 hours, or follow the manufacturer's directions. When cooking time is done, allow the pressure to reduce gradually, not under cold water.

BLACK-AND-WHITE
MARBLE PUDDING

A dense chocolate pudding combined with a delicate orange-flavored pudding. The Orange Crème Anglaise should be very cold.

SERVES 6 TO 8

3½ teaspoons plus ½ cup (1 stick) unsalted butter, softened

4 teaspoons plus 1 cup sugar

2 large eggs

2 teaspoons vanilla extract

1 cup all-purpose flour

1 cup fresh soft bread crumbs

1½ teaspoons baking powder

⅓ cup Dutch-process cocoa powder

2 teaspoons instant espresso powder

¼ teaspoon ground mace

2 tablespoons milk

2 teaspoons grated orange zest

1½ cups Orange Crème Anglaise (page 99)

Garnish

Candied Orange Zest (page 107)

Butter the sides and lid of a 1½-quart pudding mold with the 3½ teaspoons butter. Dust the entire mold with the 4 teaspoons sugar. Prepare a pot for steaming (see page 6).

Cream the remaining butter and sugar in an electric mixer or food processor until fluffy. Beat in the eggs and vanilla just until blended. Stir in the flour, bread crumbs, and baking powder. Mix on medium speed or pulse in a food processor until smooth.

Pour half of the batter in a bowl and stir in the cocoa, espresso, mace, and milk. Pour the remaining batter in another bowl and stir in the grated orange zest.

Place alternating dollops of the chocolate and orange batters in the mold. Swirl with a butter knife to create a marbleized effect. Secure the lid on the mold.

Steam on a rack over boiling water for 1 hour and 40 minutes, or until a skewer inserted in the pudding comes out almost clean. Let the mold cool on a rack for 10 minutes, or until the pudding shrinks away from the sides. Invert onto a serving platter and slice.

Nap individual plates with a little Orange Crème Anglaise and place a slice of hot pudding on top. Garnish with Candied Orange Zest.

CHERRY AND ALMOND
PUDDING

Dried cherries are just turning up in some of the markets on the East and West coasts, but if you can't find them, fresh cherries, or dried or fresh cranberries, can be substituted. When grinding the almonds, add a tablespoon or two of sugar, which keeps the almonds from becoming too pasty. This pudding is best served hot, with vanilla ice cream and any fruit sauce.

SERVES 6 TO 8

1½ tablespoons plus ½ cup (1 stick)
   unsalted butter, softened

2 tablespoons plus ½ cup sugar

1¼ cups dried cherries

¼ cup Kirsch

2 large eggs, lightly beaten

1 cup milk

¼ teaspoon almond extract

¾ cup all-purpose flour

¾ cup dry bread crumbs

½ cup ground toasted blanched
   almonds

2 teaspoons baking powder

¼ teaspoon salt

Butter the sides and lid of a 2-quart pudding mold with the 1½ tablespoons butter. Dust the entire mold with the 2 tablespoons sugar. Prepare a pot for steaming (see page 6). Plump the cherries in the Kirsch. (If you need more liquid, add a little water.)

Cream together the remaining butter and sugar in an electric mixer on medium speed, or in a food processor, until light and fluffy. Beat in the eggs, milk, and almond extract. Combine the remaining ingredients and blend them in. Drain the cherries and fold them in. Pour the batter into the mold and secure the lid on the mold.

Steam on a rack over boiling water for 1½ hours, until a skewer inserted in the pudding comes out almost clean. Let the mold cool on a rack for 5 to 10 minutes, until the pudding shrinks away from the sides. Invert onto a serving platter and slice.

PERSIMMON PUDDING

T*ry this as an unusual finale to Thanksgiving dinner.*

SERVES 8

3 tablespoons unsalted butter, softened

2 tablespoons plus 1⅓ cups sugar

½ cup diced mixed dried fruit

¼ cup golden raisins

¼ cup currants

¼ cup brandy

1¼ cups all-purpose flour

2 teaspoons ground cinnamon

1 teaspoon freshly grated nutmeg

½ teaspoon salt

2 large eggs, separated

1½ teaspoons vanilla extract

1½ teaspoons lemon juice

1½ cups persimmon puree

½ cup half-and-half

1 teaspoon baking soda

¾ cup chopped pecans

1 cup Rum Butter (page 105), or
    whipped cream sweetened with 1
    tablespoon powdered sugar

Butter the sides and lid of a 2-quart pudding mold with 1½ tablespoons of the butter. Dust the entire mold with the 2 tablespoons sugar. Prepare a pot for steaming (see page 6). Soak the dried fruit, raisins, and currants in the brandy.

Sift the flour, cinnamon, nutmeg, and salt into a small bowl. In an electric mixer or food processor, cream the remaining butter and sugar with the egg yolks, vanilla, and lemon juice. Mix in the persimmon puree and half-and-half. Dissolve the baking soda in 1 tablespoon hot water and stir into the persimmon mixture. Stir in the sifted ingredients and pecans. In another bowl, beat the egg whites until soft peaks form. Carefully fold into the batter. Pour the batter into the mold and secure the lid on the mold.

Steam on a rack over boiling water for 2 hours and 20 minutes, or until a skewer inserted in the pudding comes out almost clean. Let the mold cool on a rack for 10 minutes, or until the pudding shrinks away from the sides. Invert onto a serving platter.

Serve warm or cold with Rum Butter or whipped cream.

CARROT AND SWEET POTATO PUDDING

Although vegetables are the base for this pudding, it's definitely dessert. The sweet potato and pineapple make the pudding doubly moist.

SERVES 6 TO 8

3½ teaspoons plus 10 tablespoons
(1¼ sticks) unsalted butter

4 teaspoons granulated sugar

½ cup golden raisins

¼ cup pineapple juice

½ cup firmly packed brown sugar

3 large eggs

1 cup finely grated raw carrots

½ cup finely grated raw sweet potato

1 cup all-purpose flour

½ cup fresh bread crumbs

2 teaspoons baking powder

1½ teaspoons ground cinnamon

1 teaspoon ground nutmeg

½ teaspoon ground allspice

¼ teaspoon salt

2 slices fresh or drained canned

pineapple, cut into ½-inch chunks

¾ cup coarsely chopped walnuts

Butter the sides and lid of a 1½-quart pudding mold with the 3½ teaspoons butter. Dust the entire mold with the granulated sugar. Prepare a pot for steaming (see page 6).

In a small pan over medium heat, simmer the raisins in the pineapple juice for about 2 minutes. Remove from the heat and set aside.

Cream the remaining butter, the brown sugar, and the eggs in an electric mixer at medium speed, or in a food processor, until light and fluffy. Stir in the carrots and sweet potato. Combine the flour, bread crumbs, baking powder, spices and salt, and add to the carrot mixture. Stir in the raisins and juice, pineapple chunks, and walnuts. Scrape the batter into the mold and secure the lid on the mold.

Steam on a rack over boiling water for 1 hour and 40 minutes, or until a skewer inserted in the pudding comes out almost clean. Let the mold cool on a rack for 10 minutes, or until the pudding shrinks away from the sides. Invert onto a serving platter. Serve hot or warm.

STOVE-TOP PUDDINGS

LEMON TAPIOCA

This refreshing pudding is perfect after a hearty meal.

SERVES 4 TO 6

1 medium lemon

2½ cups milk

3 tablespoons quick-cooking tapioca

⅓ cup sugar

1 large whole egg, separated

1 large egg yolk

½ teaspoon grated lemon zest

Garnish
Mint leaves

With a potato peeler, carefully peel the zest from the lemon, making sure no white pith is included. In a heavy saucepan, scald 2 cups milk with the zest. Remove from the heat. Let cool for 10 minutes, then discard the zest. Stir in the tapioca and sugar. Let sit for another 5 minutes.

Beat the egg yolks with the remaining milk. Stir into the tapioca mixture. Cook over medium-low heat until the mixture boils, stirring often. Immediately remove from the heat. Stir in the grated zest. Beat the egg white until soft peaks form, and fold into the cooled pudding.

Spoon into custard cups or a serving bowl. Serve warm or cover and chill. Garnish with mint.

ANGEL FOOD SUMMER PUDDING

T*his sinfully rich-tasting pudding is actually healthful, since it contains no fats or egg yolks. Angel food cake replaces the white bread traditionally used in this classic British dessert. If you can find fresh red or black currants, use them in place of 2 cups of any of the other berries.*

SERVES 8

2 cups strawberries, hulled and
   quartered

2 cups blueberries

2 cups raspberries

2 teaspoons grated lemon zest

¼ cup sugar

¼ cup Cointreau

1 8-inch angel food cake

1½ cups Crème Fraîche (page 101) or
   whipped cream (sweetened with 4
   teaspoons powdered sugar)

Toss the berries, lemon zest, sugar, and Cointreau in a medium saucepan. Cook over medium heat for 5 to 8 minutes, or until the berries are soft, the sugar has melted, and the alcohol has burned off. Do not overcook. The berries should look fresh.

With a serrated knife, cut the cake into ½-inch slices and then into triangles. Trim off any overbrowned cake. Line the bottom and sides of a 1½- to 2-quart noncorrosive bowl or soufflé dish with the cake triangles. If necessary, cut pieces of cake into fingers to fit any gaps so the bowl is completely lined.

Spoon in half of the berries. Place enough cake on top to cover them. Spoon on the remaining berries, then cover with more cake. Fill in any gaps with cake so the berries are completely covered.

Place a saucer or plate slightly smaller than the bowl on top of the pudding. Weight it down with a 1- or 2-pound can, or with weights. Refrigerate for at least 8 hours, or overnight. Carefully unmold by inverting the pudding onto a serving plate. Serve with Crème Fraîche or sweetened whipped cream.

MRS. DONALDSON'S
ENGLISH RICE PUDDING

My *English friend Maureen constantly complains how much she misses her mum's puddings. This one best approximates what Maureen remembers eating as a little girl. Dried currants replace the traditional raisins, but you can use raisins if you prefer. To Americanize this dish, omit the jam and serve with whipped cream and a dusting of cinnamon.*

SERVES 6

4 cups milk

2 tablespoons unsalted butter

⅓ cup sugar

½ cup short-grain white rice

1 2-inch piece of vanilla bean, split

1 cinnamon stick

1 large egg

1 teaspoon vanilla extract

½ cup dried currants

¼ cup dark rum or water

½ cup raspberry or strawberry jam

Combine 3½ cups milk with the butter, sugar, rice, vanilla bean, and cinnamon stick in a 2-quart saucepan. Bring to a boil over medium-high heat, immediately lower the heat, and simmer for 10 minutes.

Beat the egg with the remaining milk and stir into the rice mixture. Simmer for an additional 10 minutes. Remove from the heat. The pudding may seem very thin, but it will thicken as it chills.

Add the vanilla extract, and let the pudding cool for 20 minutes before transferring to a bowl. Refrigerate for several hours, or until the pudding reaches the desired serving temperature and consistency. Stir several times while cooling.

Gently simmer the currants in the rum for 5 minutes. Let cool.

Before serving the pudding, remove the vanilla bean and cinnamon stick, and stir in the currants. Spoon a dollop of jam on each serving.

GINGERED RICE PUDDING

Though it may seem like a lot, don't skimp on the ginger.

1 cup glutinous rice or any short-grain
  Oriental rice

2 cups water

2 tablespoons unsalted butter

5 ounces candied ginger

4 large egg yolks, lightly beaten

⅓ cup sugar

1½ cups milk

1 tablespoon Noyaux (cream of almond
  liqueur)

1 cup whipped cream

Put the rice in a medium saucepan, add the water and butter, and cook, covered, until the rice is soft and all the water is absorbed (or cook according to package directions).

Coarsely chop half of the ginger. Finely chop the rest in a blender or food processor.

Combine the egg yolks, sugar, and milk in a small saucepan and cook over medium-low heat, stirring constantly, until the custard coats the back of a metal spoon. Do not allow the custard to boil or it will curdle. Let cool slightly. Pour the rice into a bowl. Add the custard, then the Noyaux and ginger, and stir well. Fold in the whipped cream. Chill before serving.

VANILLA PUDDING

Almost any additional flavoring will complement vanilla pudding. Try swirling some fresh fruit puree through the chilled pudding for a parfait effect.

SERVES 4

½ cup sugar

3 tablespoons cornstarch

⅛ teaspoon salt

2½ cups milk

3 large egg yolks

1 2-inch-long piece of vanilla bean, split

1 tablespoon unsalted butter, softened

2 teaspoons vanilla extract

In a mixing bowl, dissolve the sugar, cornstarch, and salt in ½ cup milk. Whisk in the egg yolks.

Put the remaining milk and the vanilla bean in a medium saucepan. Heat over medium heat until the milk is hot and small bubbles begin to form around the edges.

Scrape in the egg mixture. Cook over medium heat until the pudding begins to thicken and boil, stirring continuously. Cook, stirring, for 1 to 2 minutes more, or until very thick. Immediately remove from the heat; whisk in the butter and vanilla extract.

Strain into a serving bowl or individual custard cups. Place wax paper or plastic wrap directly on the surface of the pudding to keep a skin from forming. Refrigerate until ready to serve.

BITTERSWEET CHOCOLATE PUDDING WITH WHITE CHOCOLATE CHUNKS

The white chocolate chunks transform "little-kid food" chocolate pudding into a sophisticated treat.

SERVES 4 OR 5

6 tablespoons Dutch-process cocoa
   powder

½ cup sugar

2 tablespoons cornstarch

⅛ teaspoon salt

2⅓ cups milk

3 large egg yolks

1 ounce (1 square) bittersweet
   chocolate, coarsely chopped

1 tablespoon unsalted butter, cut into
   pieces

1 teaspoon vanilla extract

1 2.2-ounce bar of white chocolate with
   almonds, broken into small chunks

In a heavy saucepan, dissolve the cocoa, sugar, cornstarch, and salt in ¾ cup milk. Whisk in the egg yolks, the remaining milk, and the bittersweet choocolate. Cook slowly over medium-low heat, stirring constantly, until the pudding begins to thicken and comes to a slow boil. Cook for 1 minute more, stirring constantly. Remove from the heat. Stir in the butter and vanilla.

Pour the pudding into a 1½-quart bowl. Place wax paper or plastic wrap directly on the surface of the pudding to keep a skin from forming. Let cool, then refrigerate several hours.

When the pudding is cold, fold in the white chocolate. At this point the pudding can be spooned into serving cups. Completely cover the surface of the pudding with wax paper or plastic wrap and return it to the refrigerator. Serve well chilled with your favorite topping.

VARIATION: CHOCOLATE MOCHA PUDDING

Replace 1 cup of the milk with half-and-half. Add ½ teaspoon espresso powder to the pudding and proceed as above. Omit the white chocolate. Serve warm or chilled with whipped cream sweetened with powdered sugar.

ROTE GRÜTZE
RØDGRØD MED FLØDE
(RED GRITS)

A *thickened fruit pudding of red berries, this is a favorite in northern Germany and Denmark, where originally it was made with husked cereals, or the grits, and called respectively Rote Grütze and Rødgrød med Fløde, or Red Grits. Usually it is made with raspberries, but any combination of fresh red currants, lingonberries, strawberries, cranberries, blueberries, or blackberries is equally delicious. In New England it is called flummery when made with blueberries.*

SERVES 4 TO 6

4 cups fresh red raspberries or
   unsweetened frozen whole red
   raspberries, thawed

½ cup sugar

1 cup water

½ cup Lillet or any sweet aperitif
   vermouth

½ teaspoon grated lemon zest

6 tablespoons quick-cooking farina,
   such as Cream of Wheat

½ teaspoon vanilla extract

1 to 1½ cups heavy cream

⅓ cup chopped toasted hazelnuts

In a medium saucepan, briefly cook the raspberries, sugar, and water over medium heat until soft, about 5 to 8 minutes. Place the berries and cooking liquid in a food processor and puree. Push the puree through a strainer or fine sieve over a large bowl. You should have almost 4 cups of liquid.

Return the liquid to the pan. Over medium heat, stir in the Lillet and lemon zest and bring to a simmer. Sprinkle in the farina, stirring constantly. Lower the heat and simmer for 2 to 3 minutes more, or until the pudding has thickened and is translucent and the farina is soft. Remove from the heat and stir in the vanilla.

Let cool for 5 minutes, stir, and pour into individual custard cups or stemmed glasses or a serving dish. Chill until set. Serve very cold, topped with cream and chopped nuts.

SWEET POLENTA PUDDING

*T*his is northern Italian comfort food, best appreciated on a wintry night with a glass of sweet dessert wine.

4 tablespoons sugar

¼ teaspoon salt

3¼ cups milk

1 tablespoon grated orange zest

⅓ cup polenta (coarse Italian cornmeal)

2 large egg yolks

1 large egg

1 tablespoon unsalted butter, softened

Brown sugar

Heavy cream

In a heavy saucepan, dissolve the sugar and salt in 3 cups milk. Heat over medium heat until the milk is hot and frothy, with small bubbles forming around the edges of the pan. Add the orange zest, then slowly whisk in the polenta, stirring constantly to keep the mixture smooth. Lower heat and simmer for 15 minutes, stirring often with a wooden spoon as mixture thickens.

Beat the egg yolks and egg with the remaining milk. Pour into the polenta and cook, stirring continuously, for 5 minutes, or until the pudding is very creamy. Remove from the heat. Stir in the butter.

Pour into large custard cups or bowls. Sprinkle with brown sugar. Serve with cold heavy cream.

VARIATION: RAISIN POLENTA PUDDING

When the pudding is cooked, stir in ⅓ cup plumped golden raisins and pour into 4 generously buttered 10-ounce custard cups. Bake in a preheated 400° F. oven for 20 minutes. Let cool for at least 10 minutes. Serve warm or at room temperature, sprinkled with powdered sugar.

MARGARITA SABAYON

Margaritas are a popular prelude to a Mexican meal. For an interesting change, try ending a south-of-the-border dinner with this elegant custard.

SERVES 6

> 1 medium lime
>
> ¾ cup granulated sugar
>
> 1 cup heavy cream
>
> 2 tablespoons powdered sugar
>
> 5 large egg yolks
>
> ¼ cup white tequila
>
> ¼ cup dry white wine
>
> 2 tablespoons Triple Sec or Cointreau

Grate the rind of the lime into a small bowl, and squeeze the juice into another. Dip the rims of six wineglasses or custard cups in the juice, then into a dish filled with ¼ cup granulated sugar, coating the rims entirely. Leave in the freezer until ready to use.

In a chilled bowl, whip the cream with a whisk or in an electric mixer just until soft peaks begin to form. Sprinkle in the powdered sugar and rind, whipping until stiff peaks form. Refrigerate until ready to use.

Boil just enough water in the bottom of a double boiler so that the bottom of the top pot barely touches it. Fill a large bowl with ice cubes and cold water and put it near the stove. Put the egg yolks and remaining sugar in the top of the double boiler and beat with a portable electric mixer, whisk, or eggbeater until pale yellow, about 1 minute. Place over the boiling water. Add 2 tablespoons of the ice water and the tequila, wine, and Triple Sec. Beat vigorously over boiling water for 5 to 8 minutes, or until the mixture has tripled in volume and is very light and fluffy.

Remove from the heat and immediately plunge the top of the boiler into the bowl of ice water. Beat constantly until the sabayon is cooled. The volume will reduce slightly. Fold in the whipped cream and serve in the prepared glasses. For a firmer dessert, freeze the sabayon for 1 to 2 hours.

YANKEE BANANA-GINGERSNAP PUDDING

A baked Alaska variation of the traditional southern banana pudding. The custard used here can also be used in any recipe calling for pastry cream.

SERVES 6

2 cups milk

1 2-inch piece of vanilla bean, split

2 tablespoons cornstarch

1 tablespoon all-purpose flour

Pinch of salt

½ cup plus 3 tablespoons sugar

2 to 3 tablespoons (or to taste) dark
   rum

3 large eggs, separated

30 or so gingersnaps

3 large bananas, sliced

Heat 1⅔ cups milk with the vanilla bean until bubbles form around the sides of the pan. Do not let the milk come to a boil. Remove from heat and let steep for 10 minutes.

Mix the cornstarch, flour, salt, and ½ cup sugar in a small bowl. Add the rum to the remaining milk, and mix into the dry ingredients to form a smooth paste. In another bowl, beat the egg yolks until pale yellow. Stir into the cornstarch paste.

Remove the vanilla bean from milk and add the cornstarch paste. Over medium-low heat, bring the custard almost to a boil, stirring constantly. Lower the heat and cook for 1 minute more, or until thickened. Remove from the heat immediately. If the custard is going to sit for a while, pour it into a bowl and cover the surface with plastic wrap or wax paper so a skin does not form. (Custard can be made in advance and refrigerated at this point.)

Line the bottom of a 1½-2 quart baking dish with ½ cup of the custard. Layer about 10 gingersnaps on top. Layer a generous amount of banana slices over the cookies. Line the sides of the baking dish with gingersnaps and repeat the layers, ending with a thin layer of custard. Pudding can be finished now or refrigerated for several hours.

When ready to serve, preheat the oven to 400° F. and bring the egg whites to room temperature. Beat them at high speed, adding remaining sugar a tablespoon at a time, until stiff peaks form. Spread the meringue over the pudding, making sure to seal all edges. Bake for 5 minutes, or until the meringue is lightly browned. Serve immediately.

SAVORY PUDDINGS

YORKSHIRE PUDDING
POPOVERS

For variety, *add half teaspoon each of black, white, and cayenne pepper, or your choice of freshly chopped herbs and garlic.*

SERVES 6

¾ cup all-purpose flour

½ teaspoon salt

¼ teaspoon freshly ground white pepper

1 large egg

1 cup milk

½ cup melted unsalted butter or ¾ cup
roast beef drippings

Sift together the flour, salt, and pepper into a bowl. In a separate bowl, beat the egg and milk until foamy. Gradually whisk in the flour just until combined. Do not overmix. The batter will be thin. Let stand for 1 hour.

Preheat the oven to 425° F. Pour equal amounts of the butter or drippings into the cups of a 12-cup nonstick muffin tin or custard cups. Preheat the tin in the oven for 10 minutes, or until the fat is very hot.

Remove the tin from oven. Working quickly, pour the batter into the cups. Bake for 15 to 20 minutes, or until the puddings are puffy, crisp, and golden brown on the outside and soft in the center. Serve immediately.

GREEN CORN TAMALE PUDDING

This is a simplified version of green corn tamales, which are very popular in Southern California during the summer, when the sweetest corn becomes available.

SERVES 6 TO 8

1 tablespoon plus ½ cup (1 stick) unsalted butter

4 teaspoons plus ⅓ cup sugar

2 large eggs

¼ cup heavy cream or half-and-half

4 cups sweet corn kernels (from about 12 medium ears)

2 tablespoons flour

¾ cup yellow cornmeal

⅛ teaspoon ground cumin

1 4-ounce can diced green chiles, drained

½ cup grated Monterey Jack cheese

½ cup grated sharp Cheddar or Colby cheese

1 cup Crème Fraîche (page 101) or sour cream

Butter a 1½-quart pudding mold or two 3-cup molds with 1 tablespoon butter. Sprinkle the sides of the mold with the 4 teaspoons sugar. Prepare a pot for steaming (see page 6).

Cream the remaining butter and sugar with the eggs in a food processor or mixer until light and fluffy. Add the cream, corn, flour, cornmeal, and cumin. Process until the mixture is grainy, but not too smooth. (If you don't have a food processor, grind the corn and cornmeal together in a meat grinder and beat into the butter mixture with the cream and cumin.) Stir in the chiles and cheeses.

Scrape the pudding into the mold. Tap the mold on the counter a couple of times to settle the pudding, and smooth the top with the back of a spoon. Steam 1 hour and 15 minutes for the large mold, 35 minutes for the smaller molds, or until a skewer inserted in the pudding comes out almost clean. Let the mold cool on a rack for 5 to 10 minutes, or until the pudding shrinks away from the sides of the mold. Invert the pudding onto a platter. Serve piping hot with a dollop of Crème Fraîche or sour cream.

VARIATION

Thin 1 cup sour cream with a little milk. Combine 1 cup chopped tomato (about 2 medium tomatoes, peeled and seeded) with 1½ tablespoons chopped fresh cilantro. Pour small amount of sour cream over pudding slices. Top each serving with tomato. Serve any extra sour cream and tomato on the side.

RUTHIE'S BEST NOODLE KUGEL

*R*uthie Slutsky is my friend Debbie's mom, who lives in upstate New York. When Ruthie comes to town, we all insist she make this kugel at least once before we let her go home. Serve as a side dish with Sunday brunch.

SERVES 6 TO 8

2 tablespoons plus ¾ cup (1½ sticks)
  unsalted butter

Pinch of salt

12 ounces medium egg noodles

3 large McIntosh apples

Juice of 1 lemon

⅔ cup sugar

1 cup sour cream

1½ cups cottage cheese

½ cup golden raisins

5 large eggs

1 teaspoon vanilla extract

1½ cups crushed cornflakes

2 teaspoons ground cinnamon

Butter an 8 x 8 x 2-inch pan with the 2 tablespoons butter. Put the salt in a large pot with 2 quarts water, bring to a boil, and cook the noodles just until tender.

Peel and core the apples. Slice into half moons and sprinkle with lemon juice to prevent discoloring. Mix ⅓ cup sugar with the sour cream and cottage cheese in a large mixing bowl. Toss the raisins with the apples and add to the sour cream mixture. When the noodles are done, drain thoroughly and mix into the sour cream mixture. Melt half the remaining butter. Stir into the noodles. Beat the eggs with a whisk or in an electric mixer until pale yellow and very fluffy. Add the vanilla and stir into the noodles. Pour into the pan. Cover and refrigerate overnight. (This step may be omitted, but the texture and flavor are much better if the pudding is allowed to sit for at least 6 to 8 hours.)

Preheat the oven to 350° F. Sprinkle the pudding with the cornflakes. Combine the remaining sugar with the cinnamon and sprinkle over the cornflakes. Melt the remaining butter and drizzle over the top. Bake for 45 to 50 minutes, or until the top is golden brown and slightly bubbly. Serve hot, warm, or at room temperature.

HERBED ONION BREAD PUDDING

Don't hesitate to try any combination of your favorite herbs in this glorified stuffing.

SERVES 6

2 tablespoons plus ½ cup (1 stick)
  unsalted butter

3 tablespoons vegetable oil

3 large onions, coarsely chopped (3 to 4
  cups)

2 garlic cloves, finely chopped

½ pound fresh mushrooms, sliced

3 tablespoons chopped fresh parsley

2 tablespoons chopped fresh sage
  leaves

2 teaspoons chopped fresh thyme leaves

Salt and pepper to taste

8 slices day-old white bread, cut into
  cubes and lightly toasted

2 cups chicken stock

½ cup half-and-half

3 large eggs, lightly beaten

Butter a shallow 1½-quart casserole with the 2 tablespoons butter.

Heat the oil over medium heat in a large heavy sauté pan. Add the onions and garlic, lower the heat slightly, and sauté until wilted. Add the mushrooms, parsley, sage, thyme, and salt and pepper. Cook until the onions are translucent and the mushrooms are soft and slightly browned.

Put the bread cubes in a large bowl. Add the mushroom mixture. Melt the remaining butter. In another bowl, combine the stock, half-and-half, eggs, and melted butter, and pour over the bread mixture. Toss gently, making sure the mixture is evenly saturated. Let stand for at least an hour.

Pour into the casserole. Preheat the oven to 350° F. and bake for 30 to 40 minutes, or until golden brown and puffy. Serve as a side dish with roast chicken.

TEX-MEX POLENTA
MINI-PUDDINGS

These have always been a hit in my Tex-Mex cooking classes. You can prepare them a day or two in advance, then finish them in the oven before serving. They're terrific with chili or barbecued chicken.

2¼ cups chicken stock

¾ cup yellow cornmeal

½ cup sliced scallions

1½ cups grated sharp Longhorn
   Cheddar cheese (or mix half
   Monterey Jack cheese and half
   Cheddar)

½ teaspoon ground cumin

½ teaspoon garlic powder

⅛ teaspoon (or to taste) cayenne
   pepper

2 to 3 tablespoons unsalted butter

Bring 1½ cups chicken stock to a boil in a large pot. Mix the cornmeal and remaining stock in a bowl. Using a long wooden spoon, scrape the mixture into the boiling stock, stirring constantly. Lower the heat as you stir so the cornmeal doesn't spatter.

Add the scallions, 1 cup cheese, and the spices and cook for approximately 5 minutes, or until the mixture is thick and pulls away from the sides of the pot. Pour into 2 buttered nonstick mini-muffin tins or 9 or 10 regular muffin cups. Bang the tins on the counter to settle contents, then smooth the top and edges of the batter with your fingers. Let cool so the puddings set. At this point you can proceed with the recipe or refrigerate until ready to use.

Preheat the oven to 375° F. Butter a large cookie sheet. Loosen the edges of the puddings with a knife, turn them out of the muffin tins and arrange on the sheet so that their sides don't touch. Dot with butter and sprinkle the remaining cheese on top.

Bake for 5 to 10 minutes, or until the cheese is melted and the puddings are browned and crisp on top.

N O T E: The batter can also be spread evenly in a buttered 8 x 11-inch baking dish and allowed to cool. Turn out and cut into 12 portions before baking on the cookie sheet.

JEAN'S POTATO-CARROT KUGEL

My mother likes to add new twists to classic dishes. Here she adds carrots or parsnips to this well-loved potato pudding. The kugel is equally delicious served at room temperature or cold the next day.

SERVES 6 TO 8

5 tablespoons vegetable oil

4 or 5 large potatoes (about 1¾ pounds), peeled and grated

1 large carrot or parsnip, peeled and grated

2 medium onions, grated

3 large eggs, slightly beaten

2 tablespoons matzo meal or flour

1 teaspoon baking powder

½ teaspoon salt

¼ teaspoon ground nutmeg

¼ teaspoon (or to taste) freshly ground black pepper

2 tablespoons unsalted butter, cut into small pieces

Sour cream or applesauce

Preheat the oven to 350° F. Pour 2 tablespoons oil into a shallow 2-quart baking dish. Heat in the oven for 10 minutes.

Meanwhile, in a large bowl, thoroughly combine the remaining oil and the rest of the ingredients except the butter and sour cream. Pour into the baking dish. Smooth the surface of kugel with the back of a spoon. Dot with pieces of butter. Bake for 50 minutes to 1 hour, or until golden brown.

Cut into squares and serve hot with a dollop of sour cream or applesauce.

BRIE AND CRAB STRATA

This is my version of a recipe my friend Susan Fine used to make in the sixties, when she was learning to cook. Serve with a green salad and seedless green grapes for an elegant light meal.

SERVES 6

2 tablespoons plus ½ cup (1 stick)
  unsalted butter

8 slices day-old white bread, cubed

¼ pound Fontina cheese, grated

¼ pound crab meat, well picked and
  flaked

6 ounces Brie, very cold

¼ pound cream cheese, softened

3 large eggs

1¼ cups milk

⅛ teaspoon freshly ground white pepper

¼ teaspoon mace

¼ teaspoon (or to taste) cayenne
  pepper

Butter a 2-quart baking dish with the 2 tablespoons butter. Put half the bread cubes in the dish. Add the Fontina in one layer, then the crab, and top with remaining bread cubes.

Trim the rind off the Brie. Cut the Brie into small cubes and dot the entire top of the strata with them. (The colder the Brie, the easier it will be to work with.)

Prepare a custard by beating the cream cheese with the eggs in a food processor or electric mixer until light and fluffy. Melt the remaining butter. Beat in the milk, seasonings, and melted butter. Pour over the strata. Press the strata down with the back of a spoon so all the bread is moistened with the custard. Refrigerate overnight.

Preheat the oven to 350° F. and bake the strata for 1 hour, or until puffy and golden brown. Let sit for 5 minutes. Serve hot or warm.

CUSTARDS & FLANS

STIRRED CUSTARD

Stirred or soft custard is the basis for various sauces and desserts. It is often erroneously referred to as boiled custard. Serve alone as a cold dessert or use as a custard sauce.

SERVES 4 OR 5

2½ cups milk

4 large eggs or 7 egg yolks, lightly
  beaten

⅓ to ½ cup (or to taste) sugar

⅛ teaspoon salt

1½ teaspoons vanilla extract

Warm the milk in a heavy saucepan to just remove the chill. Take off heat. Beat together the eggs, sugar, and salt in a bowl until well combined. Strain into milk. Stirring constantly, cook over low heat until the mixture has thickened and coats the back of a metal spoon, about 15 minutes. Do not let the custard boil or it will curdle. Immediately remove from the heat and plunge the pan into a bowl of ice water. Add the vanilla, and stir until the custard is cool, to prevent further cooking. Pour into cups or a bowl and serve at once, or cover with plastic wrap placed directly on the surface and refrigerate until ready to use.

BAKED VANILLA CUSTARD

*A*ny number of delicious variations can be made by adding your choice of flavorings to this basic custard.

SERVES 6

3 cups milk

4 large eggs

½ cup sugar

1½ teaspoons vanilla extract

¼ teaspoon salt

Preheat the oven to 350° F.

Slowly warm the milk in a heavy saucepan over low heat. Do not let it boil. While milk heats, mix the rest of the ingredients together with a whisk just until smooth. Slowly pour the milk into the egg mixture, whisking as you pour. Skim off any foam.

Strain the custard into six 6-ounce custard cups or a 1½-quart baking dish. Place in a bain-marie. Bake 25 to 35 minutes for cups, 50 to 60 minutes for the baking dish, or until a knife inserted near the center comes out clean. Remove from the bain-marie and let cool on a rack before covering and refrigerating.

VARIATION: CINNAMON CARAMEL CUSTARD

Stir in ½ teaspoon ground cinnamon before pouring the custard into cups. Serve with Caramel Sauce (page 102).

BLOOD ORANGE CUSTARD

*T*his is an adaptation of a little-known Catalan dessert called Millasons.

1½ teaspoons unsalted butter

2 large eggs

2 egg yolks

½ cup sugar

⅓ cup all-purpose flour

1 cup freshly squeezed blood orange or
    tangerine juice

2 tablespoons lemon juice

1 cup milk, scalded and slightly cooled

Preheat the oven to 350° F. Butter six 6-ounce custard cups.

With a whisk or electric mixer, beat the eggs, yolks, and sugar until ribbony and pale yellow, then slowly beat in the flour and juices. Add the milk and combine well. Pour into the cups.

Bake in a bain-marie for about 40 minutes, or until a knife inserted near the center comes out clean. Let cool to room temperature, then refrigerate. Unmold and serve cold.

PEAR AND GINGER
CUSTARD

Apples also work well in this recipe.

SERVES 4

1½ pounds ripe Bartlett pears, peeled,
   cored, and cut into pieces

¼ cup sugar

1 cup heavy cream or half-and-half

4 tablespoons grated fresh ginger

4 large eggs, lightly beaten

1 teaspoon unsalted butter

Garnish

8 slices candied ginger

Put the pears and sugar in a medium saucepan. Cook slowly for about 5 to 7 minutes, or until the pears are soft. Set aside to cool. If the pears yield an excessive amount of water while cooling, drain before pureeing. Puree in a processor or food mill, then put in a mixing bowl. You should have about 1½ cups.

Scald the cream with the grated ginger in a medium saucepan. Remove from the heat and let the ginger steep for 15 minutes.

Reheat the cream just until it begins to bubble around the edges. Slowly stir ¼ cup of it into the eggs. Stir the mixture into the remaining cream and strain into the bowl with the puree.

Whisk together to mix thoroughly. Pour into 4 buttered ½-cup ramekins, filling each about three-fourths full.

Preheat the oven to 350° F. and bake in a bain-marie for 40 to 45 minutes, or until a knife inserted near the center comes out clean. Chill for several hours. Unmold if desired and garnish with candied ginger.

LEMON-SCENTED FLAN

Whether it's flan in Spain and Mexico, crème caramel renversée in France, or caramel custard in America, it's all the same soothing egg custard cloaked with an amber caramel sauce. This recipe can easily be halved.

SERVES 10 TO 12

1½ cups sugar

¼ cup water

4 cups milk

1 2-inch piece of vanilla bean, split and
 cut in half

1 2-inch strip of lemon zest

4 large eggs

6 large egg yolks

Preheat the oven to 350° F.

Combine 1 cup sugar and the water in a heavy saucepan. Caramelize the sugar over medium-high heat until light golden. Immediately pour into an ungreased 1½-quart mold, quickly tilting the mold to completely cover the bottom and sides. Set aside to cool.

In another pan, combine the milk, remaining sugar, vanilla bean, and lemon zest. Bring to a boil over medium-high heat; lower the heat and simmer for about 15 minutes, or until the milk reduces to about 3½ cups. Set aside to cool. Remove the vanilla bean and lemon zest.

Gently beat together the eggs and yolks. With a wooden spoon, stir in the cooled milk just until blended. Strain into the mold and bake in a bain-marie for 50 to 60 minutes, or until a sharp knife inserted near the center comes out clean.

Let cool on a rack for 1 hour. Cover and refrigerate until well chilled, at least 4 hours. To unmold, quickly dip the mold in hot water, then invert onto a large serving dish. Slice, and spoon some sauce over each portion.

ALMOND FLAN

T*he almonds and custard separate into layers as the flan bakes. This will keep several days in the refrigerator.*

SERVES 8 TO 10

1¼ cups plus 3 tablespoons sugar

6 tablespoons water

1 teaspoon vanilla extract

3 ounces blanched almonds

Grated zest of 2 lemons (about 1
    tablespoon)

3 large eggs

3 large egg yolks

1 14-ounce can sweetened condensed
    milk

¾ cup heavy cream

1 tablespoon amaretto (almond liqueur)

Preheat the oven to 325° F.

Combine the 1¼ cups sugar with the water and vanilla in a heavy saucepan. Caramelize the sugar over medium-high heat until golden brown. Immediately pour into a shallow ungreased 2- or 3-quart bundt or ring pan, tilting the pan quickly to completely coat the bottom and sides. Set aside to cool.

Pulverize the almonds with the remaining sugar in a food processor. Add the remaining ingredients and process until foamy. Pour the mixture into the pan. Skim off any foam. Bake in a bain-marie for 45 minutes to 1 hour, or until a knife inserted near the center comes out clean.

Let cool on a rack for 1 hour. Cover and refrigerate until well chilled, at least 4 hours. Carefully run a knife along the edges of the pan to loosen the flan and invert it on a platter. Slice, and spoon a little sauce over each portion.

RED YAM FLAN

While working on a project at the Temecula Creek Inn in Temecula, California, I met executive chef David Armour, who served a flan very similar to this unique dessert during the Christmas holidays. If red yams are unavailable, sweet potatoes, pumpkin, or any winter squash will work as a delicious substitute.

SERVES 8 TO 10

1¼ pounds red yams

1½ cups sugar

1 cup water

1 tablespoon brandy

8 large eggs

2 large egg yolks

1 14-ounce can sweetened condensed milk

1 cup half-and-half

1 cup heavy cream

1 tablespoon vanilla extract

1 teaspoon freshly ground nutmeg

½ teaspoon ground cinnamon

½ teaspoon ground allspice

1 teaspoon nutmeg

Preheat the oven to 350° F.

Scrub the yams and pierce with a fork so they don't burst while baking. Place on foil on a baking sheet. Bake for about 1 hour, or until soft. Set aside until cool enough to handle, then peel, cut into chunks, and puree in a processor or food mill. Lower the oven to 325° F.

Meanwhile, prepare the caramel. Combine the sugar with ¼ cup water in a heavy saucepan. Caramelize the sugar over medium-high heat until golden brown. Immediately pour just enough caramel into an ungreased 10-inch deep-dish pie pan, tilting the pan quickly, to barely coat the bottom and sides. Set aside to cool. Add the brandy and enough of the remaining water to cover the remaining caramel. Bring to a boil over medium heat. Simmer for 2 minutes, stirring occasionally. Remove from the heat, let cool to room temperature, and reserve. (If the sauce becomes too thick as it cools, thin it with a little water.)

Whisk the eggs and yolks until fluffy. Whisk in the remaining ingredients. Add the puree and mix just to incorporate all ingredients. Place the pie pan in an unfilled bain-marie pan. Strain the custard into the pie pan. Carefully place the bain-marie on the pulled-out oven rack and pour in enough boiling water to reach halfway up the sides of the pie pan. Bake for 1 hour and 10 minutes, or until the center of the flan is firm.

Let cool on a rack for about 1 hour. Cover and refrigerate until well chilled. To serve, carefully run a knife along the inside of the pan to loosen the flan. Invert onto a large serving platter. Cut into wedges and spoon the reserved sauce on top.

MASCARPONE CHEESECAKE FLAN

This is a very light custard that tastes just like cheesecake. *Mascarpone, which is Italian cream cheese, is available at Italian delis and specialty stores. If you cannot find it, substitute any high-quality cream cheese.*

SERVES 8 TO 10

1¼ cups sugar

6 tablespoons water

2 teaspoons vanilla extract

1 cup mascarpone

½ cup cream cheese

4 large eggs

2 large egg yolks

1 cup milk

½ cup heavy cream

½ tablespoon grated orange or other
   citrus zest

Garnish
Candied Orange Zest (page 107)

Preheat the oven to 350° F.

Combine 1 cup sugar, the water, and 1 teaspoon vanilla in a heavy saucepan. Caramelize the sugar over medium-high heat until light golden brown. Immediately pour into an ungreased 2-quart mold, tilting the mold quickly to coat the bottom and sides. Set aside to cool.

Place the cheeses, remaining sugar, eggs, and yolks in an electric mixer or food processor and beat just until fluffy. Add the remaining vanilla and the milk, cream, and grated zest, and beat or pulse several times just until thoroughly mixed. Pour into the mold. Bake in a bain-marie for 1 hour and 10 minutes, or until the top is just a little wobbly and springy.

Let cool on a rack for 1 hour. Cover and refrigerate until well chilled. To serve, carefully run a knife along the inside of the mold to loosen the flan. Invert onto a serving platter. Slice, and spoon a little sauce over each portion. Garnish with Candied Orange Zest.

MEXICAN CHOCOLATE
POTS DE CRÈME

These are best served the day they are made.

SERVES 4

1½ cups half-and-half

1 cinnamon stick

4 ounces bittersweet chocolate, cut into
  pieces

4 large egg yolks

1 teaspoon vanilla extract

2 tablespoons Kahlúa or other coffee
  liqueur

Pinch of salt

⅓ cup whipped cream sweetened with 1
  tablespoon powdered sugar

Preheat the oven to 325° F.

Scald the half-and-half with the cinnamon stick in a heavy saucepan. Remove from the heat. Stir in the chocolate, cover the pan, and let the milk sit for 15 minutes. Discard the cinnamon stick.

Lightly beat the egg yolks with the vanilla, Kahlúa, and salt. Blend the chocolate mixture into the yolks. Strain into 4 pot de crème or custard cups.

Place the cups in a bain-marie and cover with foil. Bake for 18 to 22 minutes. Do not overbake or the custard will become too dense if refrigerated. The center should be a little wobbly when removed from oven. Serve warm or cold, topped with whipped cream.

N O T E: When made in pot de crème cups, check for doneness after 18 minutes.

FROZEN WHITE CHOCOLATE POTS DE CRÈME

Almost an ice cream, these small pots de crème are the perfect finale for an elegant dinner.

SERVES 4 TO 6

1½ cups half-and-half

3 ounces white chocolate

4 large egg yolks

3 tablespoons sugar

Pinch of salt

1 teaspoon vanilla extract

¾ cup whipped cream

½ cup Raspberry Sauce (page 104)

Combine the half-and-half and chocolate in a heavy saucepan. Place over medium heat and stir constantly until the chocolate is melted and evenly incorporated.

Beat the egg yolks with the sugar and salt until well blended. Scrape into the chocolate mixture. Cook over very low heat; place the saucepan on a flame diffuser and cook over medium-low heat; or cook in the top of a double boiler over simmering water. Stir constantly with a wooden spoon, scraping the bottom and sides of the pan. As you stir, the custard will thicken, developing a lush, silky texture. The custard is ready when it coats the back of a metal spoon.

Remove from the heat and stir the custard briskly for a minute or so to cool.

Stir in the vanilla. Strain into 4 or 6 pot de crème cups (the little lids on these special cups prevent a skin from forming on the custard) or espresso or demitasse cups. Let cool to room temperature. Cover and freeze for at least 6 hours, or until very firm. Serve with a dollop of whipped cream, topped with Raspberry Sauce.

VARIATION: FROZEN ESPRESSO POTS DE CRÈME

Replace ½ cup of half-and-half with ½ cup heavy cream. Add ⅓ cup coarsely ground espresso beans (decaffeinated if you prefer). Bring to a quick boil. Remove from the heat and add the chocolate. Cover the pan and steep the mixture for 5 minutes. Stir to evenly distribute the melting chocolate. Replace the lid and steep an additional 10 minutes. Strain into a clean saucepan and continue as above. Serve with a dollop of unsweetened whipped cream, bittersweet chocolate shavings, and Candied Orange Zest (page 107).

CRÈME BRÛLÉE

B urnt cream," *the richest of all custards, presumably origi-nated in seventeenth-century England, and not France, as one would suspect. The brittle caramelized topping is a pleasing contrast to the soft cool custard.*

SERVES 4 OR 5

2 cups heavy cream

1 vanilla bean, split and scraped

5 large egg yolks

½ cup sugar

1 teaspoon vanilla extract

Garnish

Fresh berries of your choice

Preheat the oven to 325° F.

Scald the cream and the vanilla bean in the top of a double boiler. Off the heat, let the bean steep in the cream for 10 minutes.

Lightly beat together the egg yolks and ¼ cup sugar. Slowly whisk in ½ cup cream, blending thoroughly. Pour into the re-maining cream, whisking as you pour. Add the vanilla, then strain into 4 or 5 flameproof custard cups. Skim off any foam.

Bake in a bain-marie for 45 to 50 minutes, or just until custard is set. (The custard will be wobbly but will solidify as it chills.) Let cool to room temperature, then refrigerate for several hours.

Sprinkle with the remaining sugar and place under the broiler (or use a salamander, see page 12) just until the sugar caramelizes. Watch carefully. Let cool for 5 minutes, then refrigerate for 15 to 20 minutes so the custard can firm up again. To serve, garnish with berries.

VARIATION: PUMPKIN CRÈME BRÛLÉE

Add ½ cup cooked or canned pumpkin puree, 2 tablespoons cognac, ½ teaspoon ground cinnamon, ¼ teaspoon ground ginger, and ¼ teaspoon ground nutmeg to the cream and egg mixture. Serve with gingersnaps. This is best made the day before so the flavors can blend.

TOPPINGS & SAUCES

CRÈME ANGLAISE

If you prefer a lighter sauce, use whole milk instead of half-and-half.

6 large egg yolks

½ cup sugar

2 cups half-and-half

1½ teaspoons vanilla extract

Fill a bowl with ice cubes and cold water.

In a mixing bowl, beat together the egg yolks and sugar. Add the half-and-half. Cook in a saucepan over medium-low heat, stirring constantly with a whisk, until the sauce is thickened and coats the back of a metal spoon.

Immediately remove from the heat and plunge the pan into the bowl of ice water for several minutes to stop the cooking, gently whisking until cool. Stir in the vanilla. Strain the sauce into a bowl and cover. Sauce may be served hot, warm, or cold.

VARIATION: ORANGE CRÈME ANGLAISE

Add 2 tablespoons grated orange zest with the half-and-half.

LEMON CURD

Lime juice, orange juice, or even grapefruit juice can replace the lemon juice for a wonderful curd. The curd will keep in the refrigerator for about a month.

MAKES 1½ CUPS

¾ cup lemon juice

2 tablespoons grated lemon zest

2 large eggs

2 large egg yolks

1 cup sugar

4 tablespoons (½ stick) unsalted butter,
    cut into small bits

In the top of a double boiler over simmering water, whisk together the juice, zest, eggs, yolks, and sugar until frothy and lemon-colored. Whisk in the butter, a few bits at a time. Cook, whisking constantly, until thick enough to heavily coat the back of a metal spoon, about 10 minutes. Strain into a small bowl and let cool for 10 minutes. Cover and store in the refrigerator.

CRÈME FRAÎCHE

Although it's available in some gourmet stores, Crème Fraîche is very easy to make at home, and much less expensive. It will keep about two weeks in the refrigerator.

MAKES 2 CUPS

½ cup sour cream

2 cups heavy cream, preferably not
   ultrapasteurized

In a small bowl, thin the sour cream with a little cream. Combine the remaining cream with the sour cream mixture in a small saucepan. Gently heat to no more than 90° F., to take off the chill. (If you have a microwave oven, heat the cream in the container; the Crème Fraîche will culture in for about 1 minute.) Check temperature with a thermometer.

Pour into a clean glass jar, cover loosely, and let thicken at room temperature for 4 to 12 hours (It will take about 4 hours to thicken in a warm room). Cover the jar tightly and refrigerate. Crème Fraîche will have the consistency of sour cream when thoroughly chilled.

VARIATION: ORANGE CRÈME FRAÎCHE SAUCE

Add ¾ to 1 cup orange marmalade to Crème Fraîche. Stir to blend and serve.

CARAMEL SAUCE

Caramel sauce that has been refrigerated can be reheated over hot water or in the microwave.

MAKES 1 CUP

½ cup sugar

¼ cup water

2 tablespoons light corn syrup

½ cup heavy cream

2 tablespoons unsalted butter

Combine the sugar, water, and corn syrup in a saucepan. Cook over medium heat until the syrup thickens and turns golden. Lower the heat and add the cream, stirring continuously. The mixture will become very stiff. Still stirring, add the butter, and continue cooking for 2 to 3 minutes, or until the caramel is thick and very creamy. Serve warm.

BLUEBERRY SAUCE

Blueberry sauce is best when served warm. It can be refrigerated and then reheated.

2 cups fresh blueberries or unsweetened
   frozen blueberries
1 teaspoon fresh lemon juice
1/4 cup sugar
1 cup water
1 tablespoon instant flour
2 tablespoons unsalted butter

Combine the berries, lemon juice, sugar, and water in a saucepan. Cover and cook over medium heat for 5 minutes. Let cool slightly.

Puree in a food mill or food processor and strain. Return the puree to the pan. Whisk in flour and butter. Cook over medium heat until slightly thickened, about 1 minute. Serve warm.

RASPBERRY SAUCE

This *quick sauce can be made with any sweetened frozen berry pureed with a little lemon juice and sugar.*

MAKES 1 CUP

**2 10- or 12-ounce packages sweetened
frozen raspberries, thawed and
drained**

1 to 2 tablespoons fresh lemon juice

Sugar to taste

Combine the raspberries, lemon juice, and sugar in a blender or food processor and puree until smooth. Strain. Adjust sugar, and chill until ready to serve.

RUM BUTTER

Rum Butter is also known as hard sauce. It lasts for months in the refrigerator and also freezes very well. You can double the recipe and store in 1-cup containers.

½ cup (1 stick) unsalted butter, softened

1½ cups powdered sugar, sifted several times

½ teaspoon vanilla extract

2 to 3 tablespoons Jamaican rum or brandy

Beat all the ingredients together until light and fluffy. Serve at room temperature, or cover and refrigerate until ready to serve.

HELEN'S NEVER-FAIL FUDGE SAUCE

Served warm, this is a good pouring sauce. As it cools to room temperature, it naturally thickens. Reheat in a microwave oven or double boiler. If the sauce is too thick, thin it with a little cream to the desired consistency.

MAKES 1¼ CUPS

4 ounces bittersweet chocolate, cut into
   small pieces
¼ cup Dutch-process cocoa powder
⅔ cup sugar
½ cup water
2 tablespoons unsalted butter, softened

Melt the chocolate in a microwave or double boiler. In a saucepan, dissolve the cocoa and sugar in the water. Stir in the melted chocolate. Stir in the butter and, stirring constantly, slowly simmer over medium-low heat for 4 to 5 minutes. Serve warm. Store in a covered plastic container. Keeps about a week in the refrigerator.

CANDIED ORANGE ZEST

I *like to keep a supply in the freezer so I have something to nibble on when I have a sweet tooth.*

MAKES ⅓ CUP

3 medium oranges

½ cup sugar

1 cup water

Peel the zest from the oranges with a potato peeler, making sure not to take any of the bitter white pith. With a very sharp knife, cut the zest into long, narrow strips.

Dissolve the sugar in the water. Place over high heat and bring to a boil. Lower the heat and simmer until the water is clear and all the sugar is dissolved. Add the zest. Simmer for 15 to 18 minutes, stirring occasionally, until the liquid is very syrupy.

Remove the zest with a slotted spoon and spread it on a sheet of wax paper to cool completely. Store in a covered plastic container. Keeps several weeks in the refrigerator and several months in the freezer.

MAPLE CARAMELIZED PECANS

1 tablespoon unsalted butter

½ cup maple syrup

**⅔ cup pecan halves (about 2 ounces or
    40 halves)**

Butter a large platter.

Pour the syrup into a heavy saucepan and bring to a boil over medium-high heat. Lower the heat to a simmer and stir in the pecans. Cook, stirring, several minutes until the pecans are well coated and the syrup is very thick and dark.

With a slotted spoon, carefully transfer the pecans to the platter, spreading them in one layer. Let cool completely. Store in an airtight container.

PRALINE

1½ cups sugar

½ cup water

**2 cups mixed nuts, such as almonds,
    pine nuts, hazelnuts, and walnuts,
    blanched or peeled**

Combine the sugar and water in a heavy saucepan. Caramelize the sugar over medium-high heat until light golden brown. Remove from the heat and quickly stir in the nuts. Immediately pour the mixture onto an oiled cookie sheet. Let it cool and harden, about 30 minutes. Break the Praline into pieces and pulse in a food processor until coarsely ground. Store in an airtight container. Keeps indefinitely.

HAZELNUT WHIPPED CREAM

MAKES 2¼ CUPS

1 cup heavy cream

2 tablespoons Frangelico (Italian hazelnut liqueur)

2 tablespoons sugar

1 teaspoon vanilla extract

Chill the beaters and a small bowl. Place all the ingredients in the bowl, and whip until soft peaks form. Do not overbeat.

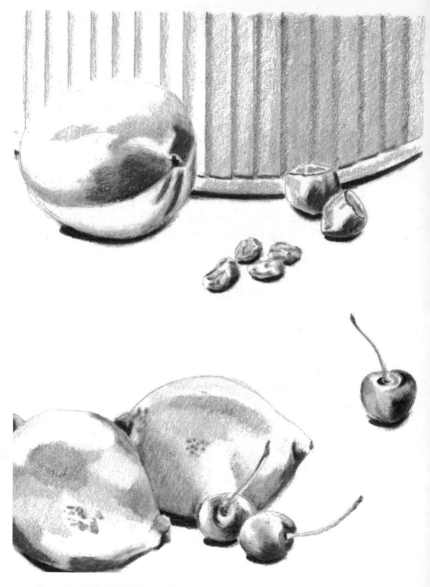

ACKNOWLEDGMENTS

Every child has a dream that spurs him or her on into adulthood. Mine, since age five, was to be listed in the Library of Congress as an author. This is the fulfillment of that little girl's fantasy.

Without the following people, this book could never have come together: Colman Andrews, who is responsible for the series of events leading up to this; my agent, Barbara Lowenstein, who thought enough of my first ideas to parlay them into realities; Regina Cordova, who unknowingly provided the inspiration; Jim Miller, who has never had a discouraging word and was the first to tell me to "write a cookbook, any cookbook"; Susan Fine, my partner in *The Food Yellow Pages*, who not only dealt with our business with a smile when I was too busy in the kitchen, but also managed to give constructive criticism, while eating pudding after pudding; Linda Burum, who, no matter the time, was always available to give encouragement and advice that usually sent me back to the stove and the computer; Maureen Donaldson, who never failed to bring me an English cookbook or pudding recipe whenever she was able; Alice Glickman, my food friend since we were twelve, who faithfully called every Saturday morning; Debbie Slutsky, who always was a willing taster; Stevie Delano, who constantly asked, "Now what are you eating?"; Peggy Mellody, whose library suddenly seemed to merge with mine; Michael Roberts, chef extraordinaire, who always provided interesting twists to what seemed mundane quandaries; my editor, Shirley Wohl, who patiently listened and then helped unravel my pudding confusion; Toni

Ringo Law, who provided spiritual inspiration above and beyond the boundaries of friendship; Helen, Dennis, and Arnie Bercovitz, whose love and endless generosity throughout the writing of this book kept up my spirits and my sometimes waning confidence; and my mother, Jean Zimmerman, who not only taught me how to make my first cookie but is the reason I always wanted to cook.

I also would like to give special thanks to David Armour, Gerri Gilliland, Mary Grigsby, Jem Grissom, Karen Johnson, Donna Hennen, Karen Lobb of the Oregon Hazelnut Board, Allan McDougall, George Morrone, Beverly Nickerson, Lauren Ryan of Dow Brands, Blair and Ron Salisbury, and Ruth Slutsky, all of whom provided recipes and information without hesitation.

INDEX